Leaving the House Unlocked

Leaving the House Unlocked

Elizabeth Enochs

This publication is made possible by funding provided by the Shaheen College of Arts and Sciences and the Department of English at the University of Indianapolis. Special thanks to the students who judged, edited, designed, and published this chapbook: Sierra Durbin and Ethan Thurston.

UNIVERSITY *of*
INDIANAPOLIS

Published by Etchings Press
1400 E. Hanna Ave.
Indianapolis, Indiana 46227

etchings.uindy.edu
www.uindy.edu/cas/english

Printed by IngramSpark

Published in the United States of America

ISBN 978-1-955521-32-1
27 26 25 24 23   1 2 3 4 5

Cover image by Annie Spratt
Cover design by Sierra Durbin and Ethan Thurston
Interior design by Sierra Durbin and Ethan Thurston
Colophon: Title is set in Sniglet Regular and body text is set in Noto Sans Light family.

Contents

Kin

Occasionally, I envy immigrant families who know exactly where they came from, how they got here, who their people are—because my own lineage isn't so clear, and I'm too paranoid to send my DNA to a company and I can't afford one of those reports anyway; what I do know is this: My family's been in southern Missouri for a long time, and I'm told before that we were in western Kentucky and northern Arkansas and eastern Tennessee—and I don't know why we left Tennessee in 1843, but it means we were Missourians when Missouri became a blood-soaked battleground torn between North and South—and it's rumored a couple of my ancestors settled in southeast Missouri after escaping the Trail of Tears, but many White immigrant families in North America pass down stories like that, desperate to believe this land is our birthright; a quick Google search tells me our surnames are mostly Celtic and English, with a touch of German or Danish, and I've been told I've got the genetic soup for alcoholism and my great grandpa sharecropped cotton and my grandpa's grandma was a child bride, and if I had to guess I'd bet we were always good with dogs and horses—but what I don't know about my kin could probably fill a library, and maybe it's better that way.

Namesakes

I carry the name of a woman I never met and a man I barely remember—a couple I know primarily through photos and stories, the former mostly black and white and sepia, the latter almost exclusively heartbreaking and infuriating—I know they died before reaching their sixties and their gravestones are etched with Masonic symbols and they left behind four adult children who rarely say anything positive about their childhoods, but I don't know if they were ever truly happy and I often wonder if my grandmother would have left my grandfather if she'd lived longer—because I've been told he beat his kids and had affairs, and my only memory of him includes being yelled at for something I didn't do—and occasionally it hits me that I'm carrying the names of two people who seem to have experienced more pain than joy during their brief time above ground, and a less optimistic person than me might consider themselves cursed to carry such a couple's names, but I've always seen it as an honor, a chance for redemption, an inspiration to cultivate as much joy and adventure and kindness as possible, no matter how much time I'm given.

Ruby's Pantry

When I think about my Zombie Apocalypse Survival Plan, which rarely happens anymore since I stopped watching *The Walking Dead* in 2016, I think about my grandma's pantry—perpetually stocked with canned beans, vegetables, and fruits when she was alive, securing it would have been my top priority once the dead rose—then I think about what it must have been like for my grandma, a child of the Great Depression and Missouri's Bootheel, to know such abundance, and I wonder if she ever opened her pantry door just to stare at the food she'd carefully chosen, bought, and put away with each label facing outward; I wonder if all that food made her feel safe or if no amount of canned peaches could quiet a deep-rooted fear of hunger, planted in infancy or perhaps even in the womb, and then I think about how I don't really know what the Great Depression was like for her because she didn't talk about it, or at least I can't remember her ever naming it specifically—I know she and my grandpa both grew up picking Bootheel cotton "until our fingers bled," and I know she was "one of the lucky ones" because she eventually got a job at a local shop while most of her siblings worked the fields for their entire childhoods—but I can't remember her actually referring to the Great Depression by name, and then I wonder if she didn't name it because it was too painful, or because she feared naming it might bring it back somehow, or if she didn't name it because she was of the "Silent Generation" and hunger wasn't even the scariest thing they had to deal with thanks to World War II and McCarthyism and polio, and then I remember my grandma was born in 1929, which means she was quite literally born into the Great Depression, and more often than not things never seem quite as bad when you don't have anything better to compare them to.

Catholic Magic

For me, New Year's Eve means remembering my grandma Dixie and the quarters she kept in a big plastic container—the kind that probably held cheese puffs before its conversion—so her grandkids could play cards and gamble; I remember her playing with us, teaching us along the way, until it was time for everyone to step outside and yell "happy new year!" while Dixie rang a small bell and ate herring and waved a dollar in the air, her traditional health and wealth ritual that always looked to my young, evangelical Christian eyes like some kind of Catholic magic, and I wonder if she saved her coins all year—slowly filling the jar after errands left her with quarters to spare—or if she visited her bank with the same request every December; I wonder who taught her how to gamble, how to summon wellness and financial stability, how to write New Year's resolutions lists—I wonder what New Year's Eve looked like when she was a young Catholic girl growing up in St. Louis, because I can't remember if she ever told me and it's too late to ask because she's in a box in the Ozarks, six feet deep and covered in roses.

My Grandpa's Grandma

I'm told my grandpa's grandma was a child bride, and I'm told her husband loved her, but I don't care how they did things in Kentucky or Arkansas or Tennessee or Missouri or wherever we lived back then—he was a pedophile and a rapist—and intergenerational trauma starts somewhere, and I'm thinking some of mine started on account of him since, you see, some scientists believe trauma can be passed down from generation to generation, like a cursed family heirloom; they say it begins in the womb, before we're even formed, but I don't understand how a child's womb was ever considered a plot to be seeded, and I wonder if she wondered the same thing, and I hope she at least enjoyed motherhood because she ended up dying for it, and I'm curious if the DNA she passed down is partly why I refuse to give birth and might never marry and don't feel safe with most men, and if it is then I suppose I'm thankful, because she's just trying to keep me safe.

Dumb Supper

I want to set a table for one hundred, decorate it with images of my ancestors, and cover it with more breads, wines, cheeses, soups, and sweets than I could eat in a month; I want to invite my parents, siblings, cousins, aunts, friends, and all the kids in my life to feast, and I want the little ones to play card games and hide and seek and whatever else brings them joy while the rest of us tell the dead about our year: Where we traveled, who we saw, how we helped, how we failed, what we ate, drank, read, heard, watched, wrote, overcame, understood, remembered, forgot, achieved, learned—I want supper to last for hours and I want there to be laughter and a blazing hearth and beloved beasts curled up in front of it, and when supper's over I want to leave the house unlocked, a tray of snack cakes by the door.

Nostalgia Becomes Grief

I want to wear corduroy overalls and tops with spaghetti straps, hear dial tones from phones with finger holes, eat gummies that gush in my mouth, drink from glasses of bonneted geese, watch 1990s VHS recordings just for the commercials, play kickball at the church playground where a girl told everyone I was queer, sneak into the sanctuary and watch myself in the Christmas play, eavesdrop on my conversations with the only Black girl in children's church, see the poster I hid under my bed so the Hansons wouldn't become a "graven image" on my wall, visit my hometown before the trailer park became a shopping center, before my first boss became my sexual harasser, before my grandparents were buried—I want to hold the dog my dad shot in the woods because we couldn't afford the vet, run from boys who made me laugh before they became men who made me cry, buy orange ice cream from a truck and stroll dirt roads with girls who became people I don't talk to anymore, walk out of rooms where adults told me how not to get raped—but more than all of that, I want to know how and why and when nostalgia becomes grief.

First Kiss

If we're talking pecks, my first kiss happened on top of a play structure when I was four years old, after a little boy from church persuaded me with the promise: "It'll be just like the movies!"—I'm told that little boy grew up to be a father, but he's been dead for a while now, and I didn't know about his funeral because we grew apart a long time ago and I don't read the newspaper, but once in a while I remember him as the little boy who gave me my first kiss, and I wonder if his short life was joyful enough, if he ever fell in love, if he managed to travel—I wonder if dying hurt or if he went peacefully, whatever that means—and sometimes I want to find out where he's buried, if he was buried, and blow kisses at his grave; but maybe it's best to remember him as the little boy who kissed little me while our parents were studying the Bible.

Superstitious

When I want people to understand what being a child in the rural Bible Belt was like for me, I tell them about following my dad around our basement, watching him anoint the corners of our home with oil before casting out demons I couldn't see or hear or feel; I tell them about tent revivals and shofars and purity rings and alter calls and hiding my Mariah Carey cassette tape and feeling the ever-present fear of fire and brimstone no matter how many times I prayed The Sinner's Prayer; but I also tell them about carrying burning sage or incense—any cleansing herb that smokes—to each corner of every place I've called home as an adult, an attempt to rid the spaces of bad memories and toxic energies; I tell them I cover bedroom mirrors when I'm sleeping in old homes or hotels or apartments, anywhere someone may have died in their sleep or had their life taken in some other way; I tell them about watching my father water witching in our backyard, about eating black eyed peas and collard greens with my grandma Ruby on New Year's Day, about honoring each full moon; I tell them I don't consider myself religious, but more often than not, religion and superstition are married where I come from—and I don't think I'll ever turn my back on the latter.

Maybe Both

Sometimes, I remember you're going to die—if you haven't already—and even if I outlive you I probably won't know when or how you die, and if I do learn of your passing it'll probably be long after you're gone, because I sure as hell won't be invited to the funeral and I don't know if I'd want to go even if I were, but I still have love for you despite the havoc you wreaked on my nervous system, despite the abuse you claim not to remember—and even though I still have nightmares about you occasionally, I still remember holding your head in my lap, too, playing with your hair, how you grinned the first time I kissed your cheek, the poem you wrote about me and morning sex, that time you carried me home, when you called me family; and as sad and sick as it is, you were my first grown-up love, you transformed me on a molecular level, and once in a while I still miss the Dr. Jekyll to your Mr. Hyde, and even though you left wounds I'm still healing, that I may never fully heal, I think I'd want to leave flowers on your grave, or spit—maybe both.

First Job

If we're not talking timesheets and W2s—rather, cash payments and biweekly visits—my first steady gig was cleaning Fran's house with my sister, and then later by myself; typically, we'd say little more than hi, bye, and thank you on those days, but Fran regularly offered sandwiches and sweet iced tea and homemade desserts when we finished cleaning, and I remember eating lunch with her at least once—I don't remember what we talked about during that meal or what her dishes looked like, but I do remember she always spoke softly and kept her hair curly and she had a stationary bike and a dead husband and a penchant for bar soap and an adult, live-in son I never fully trusted; I cleaned Fran's house for four years, and there's so much I didn't ask her—like her mother's name or if she ever left the country or which holiday was her favorite—and I can't get to know her better now, because she died years ago and I skipped her funeral.

I'll Be Damned

My dream of becoming a veterinarian died when I witnessed a declaw and an amputation on the same day and my dream of becoming an Olympic gymnast died when perfection over safety led to injuries and anxiety and my dream of becoming a famous actress died backstage during a community theater production of *The Princess and the Pea* when a grown man told 14-year-old me and all the other "ladies" to "get naked" for him, and my dream of being a famous rock guitarist died when I realized I couldn't strum for shit and my dream of being a French interpreter died when I got a B in French class and my dream of "happily ever after" has died many times—the time I remember most is him pinning me to a mattress I later burned—and my dream of building a life in NYC died when I started crying every day and my dream of being a "Company Man" died when my dream job laid me off and my dream of being debt-free by thirty died when I was hospitalized for three days without health insurance—but I'll be damned if I didn't make myself a writer, and I'd trade all my other dreams for that one.

Roadkill

Last summer, over the course of one workweek, I watched the fluffy corpse of a dog transform into bones; it's autumn now, and there are deer bodies everywhere—decomposing much more slowly without summer's heat—and it's got me wondering about roadkill, and whether Missouri pays people to clear it, because it seems to me like Missourians have simply chosen to ignore it and let the slain return to the Earth, however sad it looks or bad it smells or long it takes, but it turns out we do pay people to remove roadkill, and those bodies are either burned or taken to conservation areas, a feast for endangered wolves, rare raptors, and other protected carnivores; and speaking of carnivores, it's legal to "harvest" roadkill in more than twenty states, including Missouri, which I suppose makes sense because people are hungry and only a complete idiot would hit a deer on purpose, and it's kinder than supporting factory farms— where overcrowded animals are caged and probed and prodded and eventually slaughtered—because road-killed animals are free until the very end, but it still seems kind of gross to me, especially knowing one MoDOT worker told St. Louis Public Radio he always checks the carcasses before picking them up, since opossums and ticks and other scavengers might be inside—but gross or not, I guess learning all of this makes me feel a little less sad about roadkill; even so, I keep blowing kisses when I drive past the dead.

Vulnerable

In every state I've lived and every country I've visited, there's a list of endangered species: Mexico's Monarch Butterflies are dying thanks largely to Midwestern pesticides; Japan's Blakiston Fish Owl—the largest owl in the world—is dwindling from habitat loss; Spain's Balearic Shearwater, a seabird that roams much of the Mediterranean but will only breed on five of the Balearic Islands, is critically endangered by commercial fishing and predators; the Hawksbill Turtle, found in Bahamian waters, is essentially a dinosaur—they've been swimming Earth's tropical oceans for approximately 100 million years—but they might vanish because coral reefs are dying, and because people keep killing them for their multi-colored shells; the Ozark Hellbender, a salamander found only in southern Missouri and northern Arkansas, is endangered by habitat loss, nest disruption, death by fishing line, and an increase in fatal abnormalities we don't yet know the cause of; gaurs—wild cows with blue eyes— are becoming harder to find in Thailand; in New York's Hudson River, another dinosaur—the Atlantic Sturgeon—is near extinction, mainly due to caviar's popularity; in California, the endangered Pacific Pocket Mouse, so named for the outer, fur-lined cheek pockets it uses to carry snacks, was believed to be extinct for twenty years until 1993—all of these critters hold space in my heart and brain, but I can't stop thinking about the Snow Leopard, "Ghost of the Mountains," a wild cat who calls Bhutan home; more than 70 percent of their habitat has never been explored by humans, yet they're a "vulnerable" species, slowly disappearing from an ancient mountain range that's still somehow considered "young," and multiple nature shows and articles describe them as "elusive," so there's probably a lot we don't know about them, but we do know they have snowshoes for paws and their long, fluffy tails shield their bodies and faces while they sleep—a scene I picture nightly when I pull my blanket all the way up to my nose—and they're actually more closely related to tigers than leopards but they physically can't roar, and I can think of few things more heartbreaking than that.

Audrey

I want to tell your mother to keep you in England and I want to replace your tulip flour with stacks of pancakes and fried eggs and I want to watch you dance for the Dutch Resistance and I want to protect your brother from the Nazis and when you fall off that horse I want to catch you before you hit the ground and I want to give you hugs and lavender tea when you lose the baby and I want to tell you it's okay to leave your cheating husbands before giving them a decade of your life and I want you to know I'm so proud of you for fighting to keep "Moon River" in the film and I'm so sorry your father was cold to you and I'm happy you and Robert found each other and I've kept a picture of you in my home for years because I can think of few people more resilient than you and I know we've never met but I'm truly grateful and incredibly happy you existed.

Vivien

On a long-lost SD card, there's a photo of me sitting on a bench in Nassau reading *Gone With the Wind,* a story that used to make me think primarily of gumption—because there's no denying Scarlett's teeming with the stuff—but now instantly reminds me of slavery and marital rape, and how ironic it is that *Gone With The Wind* is the first film I remember watching in my first apartment, where I'd experience my own versions of that problematic staircase scene with my own version of Rhett—and I often wonder what Vivien thought of that scene, if something like that ever happened to her, if she felt the scene was romantic; either way I don't hate her for playing along, because Vivien died in 1967 and "I do" was tantamount to life-long consent in the UK—her Mother Country—until 1991, it wasn't illegal to rape your wife in all fifty of the United States until 1993, and even nowadays American husbands who rape their wives are often legally protected in ways other rapists aren't; hell, I was born in 1990 and I certainly wasn't brought up with the understanding that you could be raped by an intimate partner, so I'm not interested in shaming Vivien for the role she played in romanticizing spousal rape on screen—but I think I'll always wonder if that was truly her idea of romance, if she confused violence with passion off-screen as well, if most women did back then—and if the answer to all of those queries is yes, then I have nothing but empathy for her, for all of us, because women still tell me their husbands won't take no for an answer.

Josephine

I want to bring your mom muffins and coffee the day after your birth and tour 1906 St. Louis after we've eaten; I want to tag along when you start cleaning and babysitting for White families just eight years later—because I don't trust strange men with little girls and I've read you were often "poorly treated" in those homes, and I don't know what "poorly treated" entails, but your childhood must have been unhappy for you to run away from home at 13 and marry a man you'd quickly divorce—but whatever happened or didn't happen, it doesn't seem to have broken your spirit, because women without gumption don't move to Paris and perform in nothing more than a feather skirt, and they don't date other women, and they don't smuggle secret messages for the French Resistance in their sheet music and underwear, and they don't keep falling in love after love has failed them, and they don't adopt a dozen kids, and they don't refuse to perform for segregated audiences in 1950s America, and they don't join MLK for the March On Washington, and they don't earn a standing ovation at Carnegie Hall, and they certainly don't get the French to love them so dearly they're buried with military honors and given a twenty-one-gun salute; and I know you were truly as French as you were American, but I wish I'd learned about you when I was learning about Mark Twain and and George Washington Carver and Harry Truman, because no offense to those legends, but I needed a brave, femme, openly queer Missourian to look up to back then even more than I need one today.

Johnny

Lately, I've been feeling conflicted about enjoying your music, ditto hanging a picture of you—black and white, pensive, holding a cigarette that needs to be ashed—in my home since 2016, because I heard tell you hit your wife, and that would turn me off even if I wasn't a survivor of intimate partner violence, but I did some research and it seems like your wives loved you deeply, and maybe I didn't dig deep enough but I found zero articles claiming you hit them, though I did discover you and I have a lot in common: You grew up a mere two-hour drive south of my Missouri hometown, you—like my grandparents—spent your childhood picking cotton, we were both brought up Pentecostal, we've both spent time in San Antonio and Memphis and Nashville and NYC and D.C. and California, you served in the Air Force and I almost married an airman; in one way or another we're both children of trauma, and while I never got into amphetamines like you did, I understand your taste for drugs and alcohol, and I feel like I also would've given Nixon a piece of my mind if I'd been invited to the White House when you were, but you're still one of those legends I've had to rationalize my love for—your music is one of the few things my father and I enthusiastically bond over, and as soon as I can afford a record player we'll be listening to his old Cash vinyls, likely while imbibing red wine or Tennessee whiskey, maybe while munching edibles—but you were a shit father at times and my favorite song of yours, the one about Death and his Pale Horse, reminds me of my abusive ex-boyfriend, because I first heard it on one of our road trips; ultimately, though, I won't deny you were a talented son of a gun, and dead people don't profit from record sales, and my life has been full of complex, problematic men—most of whom I still have love for.

2014

I think my grandpa would have approved of his wake, because it was one hell of a party—great food, lots of booze, a little green, plenty of laughter—by nightfall nearly everyone of age was drunk, high, or both, and I can still picture kids playing with dogs and my brother playing his fiddle; it was a great send off, the perfect mix of Celtic and hillbilly, oddly fun for such a sad day, but I wish remembering my grandpa's wake didn't also mean remembering my now-ex-boyfriend behind me in the backseat of a car—him thrusting, me crying—I wish he wouldn't have kept asking after I kept turning him down, and I wish I would have kept turning him down even though he kept asking, but it might not have made a difference even if I had, and I can't undo it either way, and as cold as it was of him to leave immediately afterward, watching him drive off was a kind of gift, and as much as I might like to undo that memory, it reminds me of my relationship with my grandpa is the healthiest one I've ever had with a male-identifying human, because no other man or boy has ever made me feel as safe or as cherished as he did, and wherever he is I hope he knows how much he still means to me—will always mean to me.

2015

Near the end of summer 2015, I mortified my then-fuck buddy with the words: "As long as you're taking me out there to have sex with me and not kill me;" I can still picture him in that moment—mouth agape and speechless as he drove us through Arcadia Valley—and whenever I randomly remember that day, I always wonder what it must feel like to be utterly unconcerned the person you're sleeping with might kill you someday; you see, a report published by the Violence Policy Center presenting data from 2015 shows that Missouri—my home state, and the state where the aforementioned memory was made—had a higher-than-the-national-average rate of "female" murder victims, with 47 Missouri women being murdered by men in 2015; nationally, according to the same report, in cases where the murder weapon was known, 55 percent of murdered American women were killed with guns, 64 percent of those women were killed by "male intimates," and regardless of the murderer's weapon of choice, in murders where the victim's relationship to her murderer could be determined, 93 percent of "female" victims were murdered by someone they knew; globally, according to a United Nations report from 2015, two-thirds of intimate partner or family related homicide victims are women; personally, the man I loved and lived with for years prior to my friends-with-benefits situation, the man who would ignite a passion in me I'd never felt before slowly decimating my sense of self-worth, said he'd kill me if I ever cheated on him, hunt me down and kill me and my new boyfriend if I ever left him, even kill himself—and I'm glad it turns out he was bluffing, but I can't let go of how heartbreaking, how infuriating, it is that surviving empty threats makes me one of the lucky ones.

2019

I almost died in 2019, and I haven't been the same since—in fact, the experience was so traumatizing I'm not sure I'll ever want to return to Southern California, a place I'd fallen deeply in love with before becoming deathly ill there—but I do like to remember how unafraid of Hell I felt when faced with the very real possibility of dying, because even after losing my religion many years ago the fear of Hell lingered; to be honest, occasionally it's still tough to shake, and it doesn't help that several of my kin think that's where I'm headed, nor does hailing from and living in the rural Bible Belt make extinguishing that fear any easier, and I suppose it's also true that the living can't claim to know with absolute certainty what's next; regardless, if any of the children in my life ever ask me if Hell is a real place, I'm answering "no" without hesitation because Death is scary, but a lake of fire is scarier.

2020

In 2020, I read a news story about a mass grave dug for Covid dead on Hart Island in NYC—a city I briefly called home in my mid-twenties—and it was sometime after reading that story when I wrote, signed, and dated a homemade will in which I told my loved ones to cremate my body and sprinkle my ashes in Mark Twain National Forest—the forest that helped raise me—ideally along the path my siblings and I trekked as kids; but it turns out the mass grave I read about wasn't dug only for Covid dead, and Hart Island is a "potter's field"—a burial ground for paupers and strangers according to Oxford Languages and Google—and NYC's unidentified and unclaimed and seriously impoverished dead have been laid to rest in that dirt since the 1800s, and it's estimated a million people are buried there, and all these thoughts of burial and cremation left me curious about death rituals, so I did some more digging and here's what I learned: In Nordic cultures, the living situate coffins on top of cliffs or return their dead to nature via "death ships" placed in rivers or oceans; it's not uncommon for Tibetan Buddhists to cut up their dead and leave the pieces outdoors for critters to munch; the Malagasy people open tombs every few years to give their dead fresh wrappings and a musical dance; some South Koreans create shiny, colorful beads—which they often display in their homes—out of cremated bodies; in Varanasi, India, prior to cremation, the dead are paraded through the streets, their bodies dressed in colors signifying the virtues they held while alive; there's a Zoroastrian death tradition that involves "cleaning" dead bodies with bull's piss before placing them on top of a tower for vultures to consume; Filipino folks boast a number of unique death rituals, but my two favorites come from the Tinguian and Cavite people—the Tinguian dress their dead in fancy clothes and place them in a chair, sometimes putting a lit cigarette in their mouth once they're seated, and the Cavite people vertically entomb their dead in a hollowed-out tree of the deceased's choosing—and while I suppose I could picture my corpse in a death ship, especially given my European ancestry, I think I'd still prefer to be cremated, because dead or not I've always shuddered at the thought of being entombed or stuck in a coffin underground, and I don't like the idea of being picked at by birds or posthumously displayed, and I'm rarely happier than when I'm in the woods.

2022

As a child of the 1990s, I've lived long enough to remotely bear witness to dozens of mass shootings—hours of footage featuring terrified school children, worshippers, shoppers, massage therapists, theater-goers—it seems everyone is a target here, or at least in danger of becoming one, but it wasn't until 2022—until Uvalde, and the resulting lack of legislative action from politicians—that I realized how dissociated Americans have become out of sheer necessity; because while I can't speak for all of us, I know the weight of these bodies, these lives cut short, would bury me alive if I let them.

Acknowledgements

This chapbook wouldn't exist if not for the many creatures who inspired me to write it—long-lost ancestors, ex-lovers, creative legends, former editors, fellow writers, encouraging loved ones, all the girls and women I used to be, and all the nonhuman animals I've shared life and land with, just to name a few—but I'm especially thankful to the folks at *Complete Sentence*; my piece, "Nostalgia Becomes Grief," likely wouldn't have been written if I hadn't found Complete Sentence Lit, and their acceptance of that piece, plus the general concept of single-sentence prose, ultimately inspired me to write an entire chapbook of single-sentence, hybrid pieces that are equal parts creative nonfiction and prose poetry—so, perhaps more than anyone else, I want to thank the folks at *Complete Sentence*, who first published "Nostalgia Becomes Grief" on January 1, 2022.

A Note on Research

Perhaps more than anything I've ever written, this body of work screams hybridity: Every prose poem in this chapbook doubles as a personal essay of sorts, so there's a great deal of information in these pages sourced straight from my admittedly fallible memory; however, this collection wouldn't be what it is without the wealth of information—on everything from endangered species to generational trauma to Samhain—available online, and if you've read this far, you know sometimes telling others' stories helps me tell my own; below, I've listed the many sources I drew knowledge and inspiration from, piece by piece—the pieces that required only common sense, common knowledge, and my own recollections are not listed, for obvious reasons—it's also worth noting that I wrote this chapbook in 2021; it's completely possible some of the facts and research I've included in its pages could change over the years, particularly (and hopefully for the better) regarding endangered species and legal protections for husbands who rape their wives.

Kin:
Author: Catherine Watson
Article: "Missouri's bloody Civil War battles"
Media Outlet/Publisher: *Los Angeles Times*
Date: April 10, 2011
URL: https://www.latimes.com/travel/la-xpm-2011-

apr-10-la-tr-missouriwar-20110410-story.html

Ruby's Pantry:
Author: Not Listed
Article/Video: "The Silent Generation: Definition, Characteristics & Facts"
Media Outlet/Publisher: Study.com
Publication Date: November 24, 2014
URL: https://study.com/academy/lesson/the-silent-generation-definition-characteristics-facts.html

Author: Not Listed
Article: "Polio Elimination in the United States"
Media Outlet/Publisher: Centers for Disease Control and Prevention (CDC)
Publication Date: Original publication date not listed, page last reviewed September 28, 2021
URL: https://www.cdc.gov/polio/what-is-polio/polio-us.html

Author: Neil Howe
Article: "The Silent Generation, 'The Lucky Few'" (Part 3 of 7)
Media Outlet/Publisher: *Forbes*
Publication Date: August 13, 2014
URL: https://www.forbes.com/sites/neilhowe/2014/08/13/the-silent-generation-the-lucky-few-part-3-of -7/?sh=84f0b062c63b

Author: Josh Sanburn
Article: "How Every Generation of the Last Century Got Its Nickname"

Media Outlet/Publisher: *TIME*
Publication Date: December 1, 2015
URL: https://time.com/4131982/generations-names-millennials-founders/

My Grandpa's Grandma:
Author: Martha Henriques
Article: "Can the legacy of trauma be passed down the generations?"
Media Outlet/Publisher: BBC Future
Publication Date: March 26, 2019
URL: https://www.bbc.com/future/article/20190326-what-is-epigenetics

Author: Kathi Valeii, Medically reviewed by Adjoa Smalls-Mantey, MD, DPhil Article: "How Does Intergenerational Trauma Work?"
Media Outlet/Publisher: Very Well Health
Publication Date: Original publication date not listed, updated September 4, 2021
URL: https://www.verywellhealth.com/intergenerational-trauma-5191638

Dumb Supper:
Author: History.com Editors
Article: "Samhain"
Media Outlet/Publisher: History.com, A&E Television Networks
Publication Date: Originally published April 6, 2018, updated October 27, 2021
URL: https://www.history.com/topics/holidays/samhain

Roadkill:
Author: Karen Brulliard
Article: "Roadkill: In a growing number of states, it's what's for dinner"
Media Outlet/Publisher: *The Washington Post*
Publication Date: January 5, 2019
URL: https://www.washingtonpost.com/science/2019/01/05/roadkill-growing-number-states-its-whats dinner/

Author: Adam Edalman
Article: "'Meals under wheels': More states make it legal to eat roadkill"
Media Outlet/Publisher: NBC News
Publication Date: March 24, 2019
URL: https://www.nbcnews.com/politics/politics-news/meals-under-wheels-more-states-make-it-legal eat-roadkill-n986441

Author: Shula Neuman
Article: "Curious Luis Answers: Who Cleans Up Roadkill And What Do They Do With It?"
Media Outlet/Publisher: St. Louis Public Radio, NPR
Publication Date: April 23, 2019
URL: https://news.stlpublicradio.org/arts/2019-04-23/curious-louis-answers-who-cleans-up-roadkill-and-what-do-they-do-with-it

Vulnerable:
Author: Not Listed
Article: "Top 10 Facts About Snow Leopards"
Media Outlet/Publisher: WWF UK

Publication Date: Not Listed
URL: https://www.wwf.org.uk/learn/fascinating-facts/snow-leopards

Author: Scott Elder
Article: "Snow Leopard facts and photos"
Media Outlet/Publisher: *National Geographic Kids*
Publication Date: Not Listed
URL: https://kids.nationalgeographic.com/animals/mammals/facts/snow-leopard

Author: Not listed
Article: "More than 70% of snow leopard habitat remains unexplored"
Media Outlet/Publisher: WWF
Publication Date: May 17, 2021
URL: https://www.worldwildlife.org/stories/more-than-70-of-snow-leopard-habitat-remains-unexplored

Authors: The Editors of Encyclopedia Britannica, John P. Rafferty, Veenu Setia, Shiveta Singh, Amy Tikkanen
Article: "Shearwater"
Media Outlet/Publisher: Encyclopedia Britannica
Publication Date: Originally published July 20, 1998, last updated September 8, 2011
URL: https://www.britannica.com/animal/shearwater#ref1118749

Author: Joseph Spector
Article: "Amazing Discovery: A really old, 14-foot Atlantic Sturgeon found in the Hudson River"
Media Outlet/Publisher: lohud.com

Publication Date: Originally published March 8, 2019, updated March 10, 2019
URL: https://www.lohud.com/story/news/politics/politics-on-the-hudson/2019/03/08/amazing-catch-14-foot-atlantic-sturgeon-discovered-hudson-river/3104669002/#:~:text=Researchers%20last%20June%20using%20sonar,lurking%20deep%20below%20the%20surface

Author: Alejandro Olivera
Article: "Mexico's 10 Most Iconic Endangered Species"
Media Outlet/Publisher: Center for Biological Diversity
Publication Date: April 2018
URL: https://www.biologicaldiversity.org/programs/international/mexico/pdfs/English-Top-10-Endangered-Mexico.pdf

Author: Georgia Parham
Article: "Hellbenders: Fantastic beasts of rivers and streams"
Media Outlet/Publisher: U.S. Fish and Wildlife Service
Publication Date: Not listed
URL: https://www.fws.gov/story/hellbenders-fantastic-beasts#:~:text=The%20Ozark%20subspecies%20became%20a,threats%20affect%20the%20eastern%20hellbender

Author: Rebecca H. Hardwin, Kelly J. Irwin, William B. Sutton, Debra L. Miller
Article: "Evaluation of Severity and Factors Contributing to Foot Lesions in Endangered Ozark Hellbenders, Cryptobranchus alleganiensis bishopi"

Media Outlet/Publisher: Front Vet Sci (Frontiers in Veterinary Science)
Publication Date: February 4, 2020
URL: https://www.ncbi.nlm.nih.gov/pmc/articles/PMC7010714/

Author: Ann Alexander
Article: "Endangered species listing for Ozark hellbenders: even tough guys need protection sometimes"
Media Outlet/Publisher: National Resources Defense Council (NRDC)
Publication Date: November 23, 2010
URL: https://www.nrdc.org/bio/ann-alexander/endangered-species-listing-ozark-hellbenders-even-tough-guys-need-protection

Author: Not listed
Article: "Saving the Pacific Pocket Mouse"
Media Outlet/Publisher: Center for Biological Diversity
Publication Date: Not listed
URL: https://www.biologicaldiversity.org/species/mammals/Pacific_pocket_mouse/index.html

Author: Not listed
Article: "Hawksbill Turtle"
Media Outlet/Publisher: WWF
Publication Date: Not listed
URL: https://www.worldwildlife.org/species/hawksbill-turtle

Authors: The Editors of Encyclopedia Britannica, Dutta Promeet, Emily Rodriguez, Shiveta Singh, Amy Tikkanen
Article: "Gaur"
Media Outlet/Publisher: Encyclopedia Britannica
Publication Date: Originally published July 20, 1998, last updated April 7, 2017
URL: https://www.britannica.com/animal/gaur

Author: Not listed
Article: "Japan"
Media Outlet/Publisher: WWF
Publication Date: Not listed
URL: https://www.worldwildlife.org/ecoregions/pa0510

Author: Mark Brazil
Article: "Blakiston Fish Owl"
Media Outlet/Publisher: Japan Visitor
Publication Date: Not listed
URL: https://www.japanvisitor.com/japan-nature/fish-owl

Author: Jon Letman
Article: "The world's biggest owl is endangered—but it's not too late to save it"
Media Outlet/Publisher: *National Geographic*
Publication Date: February 5, 2021
URL: https://www.nationalgeographic.com/animals/article/worlds-biggest-owl-is-endangered-but-its-not-too-late

Audrey:
Author: Biography.com Editors
Article: "Audrey Hepburn Biography"
Media Outlet/Publisher: The Biography.com Website, A&E Television Networks
Publication Date: April 2, 2014, updated March 31, 2021
URL: https://www.biography.com/actor/audrey-hepburn

Author: Morgan Evans
Article: "A Timeline of Audrey Hepburn's Hollywood Love Stories"
Media Outlet/Publisher: *Harper's Bazaar*
Publication Date: June 16, 2017
URL: https://www.harpersbazaar.com/celebrity/latest/a10002427/audrey-hepburn-love-life-timeline/

Author: Not Listed
Article: "American Hunger Heroes: Audrey Hepburn"
Media Outlet/Publisher: UN WFP, World Food Program USA
Publication Date: June 30, 2021
URL: https://www.wfpusa.org/articles/historys-hunger-heroes-audrey-hepburn/

Author: Melissa Locker
Article: "The Story Behind Audrey Hepburn and 'Moon River'"
Media Outlet/Publisher: Southern Living
Publication Date: Not listed
URL: https://www.southernliving.com/culture/audrey-

hepburn-moon-river

Author: Maria Ward
Article: "5 Things You Didn't Know About Audrey Hepburn"
Media Outlet/Publisher: *VOGUE*
Publication Date: October 1, 2016
URL: https://www.vogue.com/article/5-things-you-didnt-know-about-audrey-hepburn

Josephine:
Author: Biography.com Editors
Article: "Josephine Baker Biography"
Media Outlet/Publisher: The Biography.com Website, A&E Television Networks
Publication Date: April 2, 2014, updated June 7, 2021
URL: https://www.biography.com/performer/josephine-baker

Author: Laura R. Jolly
Article: "Josephine Baker"
Media Outlet/Publisher: State Historical Society of Missouri (SHSMO)
Publication Date: Not Listed
URL: https://historicmissourians.shsmo.org/?page_id=4953

Vivien:
Author: Briana Bierschbach
Article: "This Woman Fought To End Minnesota's 'Martial Rape' Exception, And Won"
Media Outlet/Publisher: NPR, STLPR, From MPR News,

heard on "Weekend Edition Saturday"
Publication Date: May 4, 2019
URL: https://www.npr.org/2019/05/04/719635969/
this-woman-fought-to-end-minnesotas-marital-rape
exception-and-won

Author: Biography.com Editors
Article: "Vivien Leigh Biography"
Media Outlet/Publisher: The Biography.com Website,
A&E Television Networks
Publication Date: April 2, 2014; updated April 19, 2021
URL: https://www.biography.com/actor/vivien-leigh

Author: Lily Rothman
Article: "When Spousal Rape First Became a Crime in
the U.S."
Media Outlet/Publisher: *TIME*
Publication Date: July 28, 2015
URL: https://time.com/3975175/spousal-rape-case-
history/

Author: Neda Ulaby
Article: "When It Comes To 'Gone With The Wind,' Do
Kids Today Give A Damn?" Media Outlet/Publisher:
NPR, STLPR, heard on "All Things Considered"
Publication Date: September 25, 2014
URL: https://www.npr.org/2014/09/25/351437425/
when-it-comes-to-gone-with-the-wind-do-kids-toda
y-give-a-damn

Author: Not listed
Article: "When did marital rape become a crime?"

Media Outlet/Publisher: *The Week*
Publication Date: December 6, 2018
URL: https://www.theweek.co.uk/98330/when-did-marital-rape-become-a-crime

Johnny:
Author: Biography.com Editors
Article: "Johnny Cash Biography"
Media Outlet/Publisher: The Biography.com Website, A&E Television Networks
Publication Date: April 2, 2014, updated April 23, 2021
URL: https://www.biography.com/musician/johnny-cash

Author: Brett Johnson
Article: "The Man in Black's first wife, Vivian Cash, tells of romance, heartbreak"
Media Outlet/Publisher: VC Star
Publication Date: Originally published in 2007, published again October 26, 2016, updated September 18, 2019
URL: https://www.vcstar.com/story/entertainment/2016/10/26/johnny-cashs-first-wife-tells-of-romance-heartbreak-june-carter-vivian-cash-/92772320/

Author: Katie Knorovsky
Article: "The Roots of Johnny Cash"
Media Outlet/Publisher: *National Geographic*
Publication Date: August 13, 2015
URL: https://www.nationalgeographic.com/travel/article/the-roots-of-johnny-cash

Author: James Sullivan
Article: "10 Things You Didn't Know About Johnny Cash"
Media Outlet/Publisher: *Rolling Stone*
Publication Date: October 31, 2013
URL: https://www.rollingstone.com/feature/10-things-you-didnt-know-about-johnny-cash-78642/

2015:

Author: Not Listed
Article: "When Men Murder Women An Analysis of 2015 Homicide Data"
Media Outlet/Publisher: Violence Policy Center, www.vpc.org
Publication Date: September 2017
URL: https://vpc.org/studies/wmmw2017.pdf

Author: Not Listed
Article: The World's Women 2015 Infographics: Violence Against Women
Media Outlet/Publisher: United Nations
Publication Date: Not listed
URL: https://unstats.un.org/unsd/gender/downloads/Ch6_VaW_info.pdf

2020:

Author: Meg Anderson
Article: "Burials On New York Island Are Not New, But Are Increasing During Pandemic"
Media Outlet/Publisher: NPR
Publication Date: April 10, 2020
URL: https://www.npr.org/sections/coronavirus-live-updates/2020/04/10/831875297/burials-on-new-

york-island-are-not-new-but-are-increasing-during-pandemic

Author: Tim Newcomb
Article: "7 Unique Burial Rituals Across the World"
Media Outlet/Publisher: Encyclopedia Britannica
Publication Date: Not Listed
URL: https://www.britannica.com/list/7-unique-burial-rituals-across-the-world

Author: Daniel E. Slotnik
Article: "Up to a tenth of New York City's coronavirus dead may be buried in a potter's field"
Media Outlet/Publisher: The New York Times
Publication Date: March 25, 2021
URL: https://www.nytimes.com/2021/03/25/nyregion/hart-island-mass-graves-coronavirus.html

About Etchings Press

Etchings Press is a student-run publisher at the University of Indianapolis that runs a post-publication award—the Whirling Prize—as well as an annual publication contest for one poetry chapbook, one prose chapbook, and one novella. On occasion, Etchings Press publishes new chapbooks from previous winners. For more information about these contests and the Whirling Prize post-publication award, please visit etchings.uindy.edu.

Poetry

2023: *Other Side of Sea* by Xiaoqiu Qiu
2022: *A Place That Knows You* by Tiwaladeoluwa Adekunle
2022: *The Vaudeville Horse* by Elizabeth Kerlikowske
2021: *My Mother's Ghost Scrubs the Floor at 2 a.m.* by Robert Okaji
2020: *Vaginas Need Air* by Tori Grant Welhouse
2019: *As Lovers Always Do* by Marne Wilson
2018: *In the Herald of Improbable Misfortunes* by Robert Campbell
2017: *Uncle Harold's Maxwell House Haggadah* by Danny Caine
2016: *Some Animals* by Kelli Allen
2015: *Velocity of Slugs* by Joey Connelly
2014: *Action at a Distance* by Christopher Petruccelli

Prose

2023: *Leaving the House Unlocked* by Elizabeth Enochs (non-fiction)
2022: *Triple Point* by Laura Story Johnson (essays)
2021: *Bad Man Love Stories* by Curtis VanDonkelaar (fiction)
2020: *Three in the Morning and You Don't Smoke Anymore* by Peter J. Stavros (fiction)

2019: *Dissenting Opinion from the Committee for the Beatitudes* by Marc J. Sheehan (fiction)
2018: *The Forsaken* by Chad V. Broughman (fiction)
2017: *Unravelings* by Sarah Cheshire (memoir)
2016: *Pathetic* by Shannon McLeod (essays)
2015: *Ologies* by Chelsea Biondolillo (essays)
2014: *Static: Stories* by Frederick Pelzer (fiction)

Novella
2023: *Our Cadaver* by Elizabeth Toman
2022: *Goodbye to the Ocean* by Susan L. Lin
2021: *Miss Alma May Learns to Fight* by Stuart Rose
2020: *Under Black Leaves* by Doug Ramspeck
2019: *Savonne, Not Vonny* by Robin Lee Lovelace
2018: *Edge of the Known Bus Line* by James R. Gapinski
2017: *The Denialist's Almanac of American Plague and Pestilence* by Christopher Mohar
2016: *Followers* by Adam Fleming Petty

Chapbooks from Previous Winners
2022: *slighted...* by Chad V. Broughman (fiction)
2020: *Fruit Rot* by James R. Gapinski (fiction)
2016: *#LOVESONG* by Chelsea Biondolillo (microessays with photos and found text)

Elizabeth "Liz" Enochs is a queer writer from southeast Missouri. More often than not, you'll find her in the woods. To read more of Liz's writing, visit her website: elizabethenochs.com.

CPSIA information can be obtained
at www.ICGtesting.com
Printed in the USA
BVHW092323090623
665686BV00026B/1554